Jesus
REDISCOVERED

Who do you say that He is?

WEEK ONE

Jesus according to
OUR CULTURE

"Presumed familiarity [with Jesus] has led to unfamiliarity. Unfamiliarity has led to contempt. Contempt has led to profound ignorance." **Dallas Willard**

Politician

Moral teacher

Vending machine

Personal life coach

Do any of these cultural ideas resonate with how you view Jesus?

Have you encountered other cultural ideas about Jesus that aren't listed?

Jesus according to

HIMSELF

Only Savior

"The Son of Man came to seek and to save the lost." **Luke 19:10**

Only Way

"I am the way, and the truth, and the life. No one comes to the Father except through me." **John 14:6**

Only King

"All authority in heaven and on earth has been given to me." **Matthew 28:18**

God

"I and the Father are one." John 10:30

Which of these claims of Jesus is easiest for you to accept? Hardest?

Based on what we have covered, why is a person's response to the true Jesus an important decision?

SUMMARY

If Jesus is right, we are separated from God and doomed as sinful humans. Jesus is the only way to be made right with God. So knowing Jesus isn't merely a matter of agreeing to some abstract religious truths. Knowing Jesus can't be boiled down so simply moral living or to a political identification. Knowing and following the true Jesus is a matter of eternal life and death.

WEEK
TWO

Who is GOD?

Describe your view of God. What influences have shaped your view of God?

The Creator

In the beginning, God created the heavens and the earth. **Genesis 1:1**

The King

For the Lord is a great God, and a great King above all gods. **Psalm 95:3**

Just and forgiving

The Lord passed before him and proclaimed, "The Lord, the Lord, a God merciful and gracious, slow to anger, and abounding in steadfast love and faithfulness, keeping steadfast love for thousands, forgiving iniquity and transgression and sin, but who will by no means clear the guilty, visiting the iniquity of the fathers on the children and the children's children, to the third and the fourth generation." **Exodus 34:6-7**

Who are
WE?

Are all humans basically good? Explain your answer and why you think the way you do.

Made for relationship and rule

Then God said, "Let us make man in our image, after our likeness. And let them have dominion over the fish of the sea and over the birds of the heavens and over the livestock and over all the earth and over every creeping thing that creeps on the earth." [...] And God blessed them. And God said to them, "Be fruitful and multiply and fill the earth and subdue it, and have dominion over the fish of the sea and over the birds of the heavens and over every living thing that moves on the earth."
Genesis 1:26, 28

Made to trust and obey God

And the Lord God commanded the man, saying, "You may surely eat of every tree of the garden, but of the tree of the knowledge of good and evil you shall not eat, for in the day that you eat of it you shall surely die."
Genesis 2:16-17

What have we
BECOME?

Rebels who self-rule

Therefore, just as sin came into the world through one man, and death through sin, and so death spread to all men because all sinned. **Romans 5:12**

Sinners at heart

For from within, out of the heart of man, come evil thoughts, sexual immorality, theft, murder, adultery, coveting, wickedness, deceit, sensuality, envy, slander, pride, foolishness. All these evil things come from within, and they defile a person. **Mark 7:21-23**

Do these truths about human nature match or conflict with your view of yourself? Explain.

◆

Can we make ourselves

RIGHT WITH GOD?

The Lord looks down from heaven on [humanity], to see if there are any who understand, who seek after God. They have all turned aside; together they have become corrupt; there is none who does good, not even one. **Psalm 14:2-3**

According to God, can "being a good person" (defined according to human standards) make a person right with God? Explain.

For the wages of sin is death. **Romans 6:23**

Because God is just, He gives humans what we have earned. According to Romans 6:23, what has our sinful rebellion earned?

Are we in need of a savior? Explain.

If you were seriously ill, would you want your doctor to explain your diagnosis with honest accuracy? Why is it important that we have an honestly accurate diagnosis of our spiritual condition? How can an accurate (though difficult) diagnosis actually be an expression of love?

SUMMARY

As Creator, God is the King over all He made. God made humans for relationship with Himself. If humans trusted and obeyed Him they would share His rule over the world. But when humans listened to Satan, the serpent, they sinfully distrusted and disobeyed God. Instead of being godly rulers, they became enslaved to sin and Satan. Instead of being God's representative rulers, humans became enemy rebels against God doomed to eternal death apart from God.

WEEK THREE

Gospel means

GOOD NEWS

What is the good news about

JESUS?

He established God's rule.

[Jesus] will be great and will be called the Son of the Most High. And the Lord God will give to him the throne of his father David, and he will reign over the house of Jacob forever, and of his kingdom there will be no end." **Luke 1:23-33**

He brought healing.

And the Pharisees and their scribes grumbled at his disciples, saying, "Why do you eat and drink with tax collectors and sinners?" And Jesus answered them, "Those who are well have no need of a physician, but those who are sick. I have not come to call the righteous but sinners to repentance." **Luke 5:30-32**

He paid our sin-penalty.

For Christ also suffered once for sins, the righteous for the unrighteous, that he might bring us to God. **1 Peter 3:18**

He resurrected to defeat death.

For as by a man [Adam] came death, by a man [Jesus] has come also the resurrection of the dead. For as in Adam all die, so also in Christ shall all be made alive. **1 Corinthians 15:21-22**

He is enthroned as the King.

...now [God] commands all people everywhere to repent, because he has fixed a day on which he will judge the world in righteousness by [Jesus] whom he has appointed; and of this he has given assurance to all by raising him from the dead. **Acts 17:30-31**

What parts of the good news about Jesus are familiar to you? Which are new or confusing?

Why is this message about King Jesus good news that changes the world?

He will return to fully heal our sin-broken world.

"Behold, the dwelling place of God is with man. He will dwell with them, and they will be his people, and God himself will be with them as their God. He will wipe away every tear from their eyes, and death shall be no more, neither shall there be mourning, nor crying, nor pain anymore, for the former things have passed away." [...] "Behold, I am making all things new." **Revelation 21:3-5**

How does Jesus's death make us

RIGHT WITH GOD?

For our sake he made him to be sin who knew no sin, so that in him we might become the righteousness of God. **2 Corinthians 5:21**

Why was it necessary for Jesus to graciously die for our sins rather than us try to change and be good enough for God?

For by grace you have been saved through faith. And this is not your own doing; it is the gift of God, not a result of works, so that no one may boast. **Ephesians 2:8-9**

Is there anything we can do to earn favor with King Jesus?

What do you think a proper response to this good news should look like?

SUMMARY

As the God-sent rescuing King, Jesus lived the life we cannot. He perfectly trusted and obeyed God, the Father. Jesus died the death we deserve. He died to pay our sin-penalty to God and to free us from enslavement to sin and Satan. He rose again to defeat death for us. And he was enthroned to reclaim and rule over the world God made. As the forgiving King, he calls all rebellious humans to turn from sin and self-rule to trust and follow him as King.

WEEK FOUR

How does a person
RESPOND?

Repent and believe in the gospel. **Mark 1:15**

◆

What is

REPENTANCE?

Repentance is when a person owns his guilt for sin against God, hates his sin, and casts himself on God's mercy.

He also told this parable to some who trusted in themselves that they were righteous, and treated others with contempt: "Two men went up into the temple to pray, one a Pharisee and the other a tax collector. The Pharisee, standing by himself, prayed thus: 'God, I thank you that I am not like other men, extortioners, unjust, adulterers, or even like this tax collector. I fast twice a week; I give tithes of all that I get.' But the tax collector, standing far off, would not even lift up his eyes to heaven, but beat his breast, saying, 'God, be merciful to me, a sinner!' I tell you, this man went down to his house justified, rather than the other. For everyone who exalts himself will be humbled, but the one who humbles himself will be exalted." **Luke 18:9-14**

What is
FAITH?

Faith is trust in God, who declares repentant sinners fully forgiven and accepted.

Now to the one who works, his wages are not counted as a gift but as his due. And to the one who does not work but believes in him who justifies the ungodly, his faith is counted as righteousness. **Romans 4:4-5**

According to Romans 4:4-5, does God only save people who "clean up their lives" and work to earn God's approval? If not, who does God save (according to these verses)?

What results from

REPENTANCE AND FAITH?

Freedom

[Jesus told Paul to preach the gospel to people] to open their eyes, so that they may turn from darkness to light and from the power of Satan to God...

Forgiveness

...that they may receive forgiveness of sins...

Fellowship

...and a place among those who are [specially devoted] by faith in me. **Acts 26:18**

Following

And Jesus came and said to [His messengers], "All authority in heaven and on earth has been given to me. Go therefore and make disciples of all nations, baptizing them in the name of the Father and of the Son and of the Holy Spirit, teaching them to observe all that I have commanded you. **Matthew 28:18-20**

How does this explanation of becoming a Christian compare to how you have understood what it means to become a Christian?

The cost and gain of
FOLLOWING JESUS

Devotion

Whoever loves father or mother more than me is not worthy of me, and whoever loves son or daughter more than me is not worthy of me. And whoever does not take his cross and follow me is not worthy of me. Whoever finds his life will lose it, and whoever loses his life for my sake will find it. **Matthew 10:37-39**

Sacrifice

For which of you, desiring to build a tower, does not first sit down and count the cost, whether he has enough to complete it? Otherwise, when he has laid a foundation and is not able to finish, all who see it begin to mock him, saying, 'This man began to build and was not able to finish.' Or what king, going out to encounter another king in war, will not sit down first and deliberate whether he is able with ten thousand to meet him who comes against him with twenty thousand? And if not, while the other is yet a great way off, he sends a delegation and asks for terms of peace. So therefore, any one of you who does not renounce all that he has cannot be my disciple. **Luke 14:28-33**

Following Jesus means unending life in fellowship with God and a promised place ruling over the renewed creation with God (like we were created for originally).

And this is eternal life, that they know you, the only true God, and Jesus Christ whom you have sent. **John 17:3**

[This is a description of the new creation God will make:] "Behold, the dwelling place of God is with man. He will dwell with them, and they will be his people, and God himself will be with them as their God. He will wipe away every tear from their eyes, and death shall be no more, neither shall there be mourning, nor crying, nor pain anymore, for the former things have passed away." [...] and they will reign forever and ever. **Revelation 21:3-4, 22:5**

What is promised to those who trust and follow Jesus?

Have you already turned from sin and self-rule to consciously trust and follow Jesus as your King? If not, do you want to begin your journey of following Jesus now?

Made in United States
Troutdale, OR
02/05/2024

17474907R00017